THE CAREER LIFE CYCLE

Navigating the 5 Stages of Work Success

CHARLES L. JONES

The Career Life Cycle: Navigating the 5 Stages of Work Success

Published by StoryBuilders Press

Paperback: 978-1-954521-14-8
Ebooklet: 978-1-954521-15-5

I dedicate this book as a blueprint and playbook for those people who are seeking knowledge on how to successfully navigate the stages in their career. Even though the struggle is real, I hope it inspires you to believe in yourself and understand that the only courage you need is the courage to follow your own dream.

TABLE OF CONTENTS

Chapter 1: Taking Charge of Your Career 1
Chapter 2: Stage 1—Exploration 13
Chapter 3: Stage 2—Establishment 25
Chapter 4: Stage 3—Elevation 35
Chapter 5: Stage 4—Enrichment 43
Chapter 6: Stage 5—Exit 51
Chapter 7: Final Thoughts 59

About the Author 61

CHAPTER 1

TAKING CHARGE OF YOUR CAREER

As a child, I had a vivid dream one night of being a grown-up important businessman, wearing a dark suit and tie, with round eyeglasses and a salt-and-pepper gray beard. I figured I was pretty wealthy, because I was standing in front of a really nice car—a wood-paneled station wagon! When I woke up and shared that dream with my father, he said to me, "I know one day you're going to do big things!"

When we're young, we dream of the career we will have when we grow up. Whether it's becoming a doctor, a lawyer, a teacher, an astronaut, a professional athlete, a firefighter, a minister, or an important business person, we all have those dreams. Little do we know as children that, on average, we will each have 12 careers in our professional life. In 2020 alone, 37% of the workforce was laid off or changed jobs. At any time, an average of 65% of workers are pursuing a different career, which makes sense with the average time with a single employer at 4.1 years.

Maybe today you're just starting out on a career path and could use some guidance as to what to expect. Or maybe you find yourself in the position of wanting to advance in your career, but you feel stuck and can't seem to jump the gap that keeps you from getting to that next level. You might feel held back by ethnicity, gender, sexual orientation, family, personal challenges, your education or lack thereof, and any number of reasons.

Or maybe you just feel like your company doesn't care about you or your best interest. Well, here's a newsflash: Your company actually *doesn't* love you. And you shouldn't expect them to.

It's not their job to manage your career—and that's good news. Your career growth, advancement, position, or any success you're going to achieve is 100 percent in your hands.

Does that surprise you? Does it shock you to think that you have the ability to advance your career? How does it feel to know you're not at the mercy of your corporate circumstances, and the direction of your career is in your hands?

Maybe you can relate to the results of a recent nationwide survey of U.S. workers that revealed 46% of workers are *dissatisfied* with their employment. Survey participants gave weak marks to the most important driver of job satisfaction: their current job's potential for future growth. Do the math—that's almost one out of every two people who feels underappreciated, underutilized, just plain stuck, or trapped in a dead-end career. Other complaints included lack of communication, unfair pay, favoritism, overwork, micromanagement, and overbearing or incompetent managers.

Do any of these complaints sound familiar? Believe me, I get it. At one time or another in my career, I've felt the frustration of most of these situations. But as I reflect back on my experiences, I understand that every mistake, setback, and test I faced was necessary for me to take ownership of my career journey.

Been There, Done That

When it comes to climbing the corporate ladder, I've been there, done that. My career path began in military leadership before transitioning to corporate leadership, and it culminated in my becoming a Human Resources Business Lead for North America Sales in Mondelez International (formerly Kraft Foods).

That's a long way to travel for a dark-skinned African American man, born in the mid-1960s during the Civil Rights Movement and raised in rural and poverty-stricken Mississippi. The odds of graduating from college, serving as an officer in the military during wartime, retiring as an executive from a Fortune 100 company, and starting a consulting business were, quite frankly, too far-fetched to have ever imagined when I was a young man. It was simply taboo in those days to dare to dream big.

But I didn't let that stop me. I attended Jackson State University on an ROTC scholarship. I joined that program initially thinking it was a way to get an easy *A*. I quickly learned that would not be the case, but I did work hard and graduated from the program with honors and a degree in Finance. I was also blessed to meet my wife, Bobbie, a fellow Finance major, during that time.

After graduating, I became a Second Lieutenant in the U.S. Army and graduated #1 in Officer School. I was honored to be one of only a few African-American men selected to serve as an officer in the U.S. 1st Cavalry Division—yes, the same unit that George Custer commanded in the 1800s!

I was promoted to First Lieutenant in 1988 and assigned as the Air Defense Artillery Executive Officer at Fort Hood, where I was second in command and responsible for four platoons. Part of that job involved writing battle plans, so when the first Gulf War (Desert Storm) happened in mid-1990, my unit went to Iraq as an advance party to develop battle plans, pre-position supplies, and handle other support logistics before the rest of the troops arrived.

In January 1991, I was promoted to Captain and assumed the responsibilities associated with commanding, leading, and managing soldiers. I returned to the U.S. in September of 1991.

My first daughter was born only three weeks before my initial deployment to Iraq, so by the time I returned home, she had already celebrated her first birthday. With my new daughter in mind, I knew I wouldn't stay in the military much longer, because I recognized the stress it would create for my family long-term and didn't want that for my life.

I asked to be transferred out of the all-male, combat arms units and into the Quartermaster Corps to stay closer to home. This unit more closely resembled the diverse makeup of corporate America, and I thought switching to this unit would better help me to assimilate into the "real world" and prepare for what I knew would be my exit strategy from the military. Within two years, I was offered a corporate leadership position.

After serving my country for six years in both peacetime and war, I began my corporate career with Kraft Foods, now Mondelez International. I was selected for a management training program that, combined with my persistence and hard work, resulted in a promotion about every two years.

Before I retired in 2018, I held ten positions of increasing responsibility with commensurate salary and benefits. In my final position, I was responsible for Human Resources Leadership for 5,000 sales associates and leaders across America and helped drive total revenue of $2.5 billion.

Your Career Life Cycle

In my work with Kraft, I spent a lot of time thinking about the "product life cycle." When a product enters the market, it has a life cycle that carries it from being new and useful to eventually being retired out of circulation from the market. This process happens continually, taking products from their introductory stages all the way through their decline and eventual retirement. (Kraft's Trolli Road Kill, a fruit-flavored gummy candy shaped like flattened dead animals, is one example that sped through the cycle quickly.)

An *aha* moment happened for me when I realized that a career follows a similar cycle—but most people don't realize it. In fact, the typical career has five career stages everyone must go through to succeed, whether at one company or—more likely—a number of companies.

I call it the **Career Life Cycle.** The stages are…

1. **Exploration**
2. **Establishment**
3. **Elevation**
4. **Enrichment**
5. **Exit**

I navigated each of the five stages while at the same company in Corporate America, but that isn't always the case for everyone. People change employers more frequently now, rarely staying with the same company for the duration of their career. The Career Life Cycle also applies in fields outside of traditional businesses, including medicine and academia, where ascending the ranks often requires development of niche and production to ascend (i.e. degrees such as MD, PhD, Masters).

As you assess your status at each stage of your career, you may need to course-correct when necessary, seek a new job, or make a career change, especially if you are a new entrant in the workforce with less than five years of experience. And there is always the reality that a company may not be a good fit for you at any stage. You have to be willing to be flexible but not run from challenges.

There is absolutely nothing wrong with exploring new opportunities and job-hopping as you pursue your career path. You are the CEO of your own career, so you get to make that call. However, the sooner you find your passion and locate a company that fits you and your goals the best, the sooner you can get established and build a foundation to jump-start your career.

If you're just starting out in your career, you may envision climbing that corporate ladder quickly, skipping rungs as you go, fast-tracking to the top. But there is a process to be followed to get there. When you understand the process, you can engage it with purpose. You can prepare for the next stage and lay a foundation for a fulfilling retirement, rather than being forced into obsoletion and decline.

You can position yourself to live the life you want to live once your time in the corporate world is complete, while also enjoying every phase of your career journey by following these five stages:

1. Exploration

The exploration stage is the early employment time where people have recently entered the workforce. At this point, it's about discovery, self-promoting, individualism, and learning from failures. Oftentimes, they've created several fantasies and unrealistic expectations about what comes next. That's normal. But a common mistake made during this stage is to be impatient, subscribing to the "I Want It Now" mantra of instant gratification. No, you are not ready to lead the company immediately after you finish school and get started in the workforce. It's great to be confident, but equally great to embrace humility and realize you have a lot to learn. In some fields, entering the exploration stage feels like being thrown in the deep end with all that you have to learn, and that may require sacrificing social time with family and friends as you soak it all up.

2. Establishment

At this critical stage, it's about applying what you have discovered in the exploration stage. You'll often be given opportunities to demonstrate learning agility, to make mistakes, to deliver results, to lead at different levels, and to receive promotions with greater responsibility. This stage requires you to build effective teams and achieve results through others. It's about the collective us and we, not I or me. In some cases, you may be assigned a mentor or coach to assist in your career development and advancement—but not always. You may need to seek out support.

Receiving feedback from others is important; if you don't, it's possible your development can be hindered. During this critical time, you'll plan ahead and take steps that look further down the road. For example, you might look into retirement planning, rather than postponing it until later in your career.

3. Elevation

At this stage, you've been in the game long enough to understand how it's played and should have earned a seat at the table. In most cases, it's simply unacceptable to consistently fail to deliver results or to add value to the company daily.

By now you should have clearly embraced the reality that you are the CEO of your own career. You should ask yourself where your ceiling is and what's your motivation. You may be receiving offers from other companies; as a result you have to determine if you're going to stay with the company or leave for different reasons (for example: larger salary, higher level position, or due to a change in your priorities. You've probably been assigned a sponsor and should have been placed on the Succession Plan to be promoted to at least two levels above your current salary grade.

If you've done the work, connected with people, and delivered results, you're probably considered to be high-performing, high-potential, and a top talent at the company. If it's not working out for you, maybe it's time to consider employment elsewhere. You realize it's not about loyalty; it's about reaching your highest potential.

At this stage, it's essential to balance career and personal life, because it's likely a lot will be asked of you in both directions, creating competing commitments. Your retirement plan should be well on its way utilizing wealth building strategies like 401k, stocks, and personal savings.

4. Enrichment

During the Enrichment stage, you begin to face reality. You should ask yourself how far it's possible for you to go. Usually, by this point, you'll reach the highest attainable position based on your career trajectory and promotability within the company. Unfortunately, in most cases, position and salary stagnation occurs due to limited advancement opportunities. If you haven't yet met with a financial advisor, it's time! By this point, you need to know your retirement savings goals in both the dollar amount and the year you're shooting for. A trusted and certified financial planner will help you make sure you're where you should be.

Also during this career peak, you should become a mentor to help guide others through their career experiences and challenges. At this stage, it's important to do reverse mentoring. Find that younger person who can teach you a thing or two, enriching you with a new perspective. You'll also begin to prepare for life after your corporate career, laying the foundation for the post-retirement life you want to live.

5. Exit (or Decline)

You have a choice at this stage. You can either prepare to exit with dignity and on your own terms, or you can ignore the Career Life Cycle and slip into decline.

In the Exit stage, the decision has been made, either by you or the company, that it is time to part ways, voluntarily or involuntarily. If you're not prepared to step away from your corporate career and into what's next, this can be the most difficult stage, but it doesn't have to be.

It certainly wasn't for me. You may choose to retire, or you may decide to reinvent yourself to remain viable in the workforce. The point is, by following the Career Life Cycle and the advice I'll give you in the pages to follow, you'll have the power to choose—because you are the CEO of your own career!

Paying it Forward

Over the course of more than 30 years climbing the ladder in corporate America, I came to understand these five stages. I learned that there are key lessons, defining moments, and life-changing events that occur when you are chasing the American Dream—and they are transferable, not only among corporate positions, but into other fields as well. You can learn and apply them to your own journey, to pursue your own version of that dream. You don't need to live an unfulfilled life or be stuck in a career you don't want. With a little preparation and planning, you can control your own success.

Against all odds, I survived and conquered my Career Life Cycle. That's not to say it was always easy, or that it will be easy for you. You'll need to make sacrifices, just as I did. But when you engage the process intentionally, you'll enjoy a satisfying and lucrative career, maybe at one company, but more likely across a few different companies.

It is my desire—my obligation—to pay it forward by sharing my journey, from humble beginnings to career success, and the practical life experiences and lessons that shaped my professional path and personal fulfillment. In the pages that follow, I'll share practical life lessons, both empirical and anecdotal, that you can apply while navigating through the pitfalls and landmines of an ever-changing corporate battlefield.

If you apply the lessons I learned—sometimes the hard way—that are shared in the upcoming chapters, you will be well-positioned to achieve the highest potential in your own career.

You'll be able to measure your progress through each of The Career Life Cycle stages, avoid frustration, gain clarity on your direction, and ultimately exit on your own terms, financially secure and satisfied with a job well done. You'll be ready to enjoy the fruits of your labor.

Your career is in your hands, just as it was in my hands as a young man just starting out so many years ago. But will you accept the responsibility to be the CEO of your own career? I hope so, because whether you realize it or not, you already are.

CHAPTER 2

STAGE 1—EXPLORATION

In August of 1987, after graduating as the #1 Officer in the Air Defense Officers Basic Course, I reported for duty as a Platoon Leader in the 1st Cavalry Division at Ft. Hood, Texas. In many ways, it was the beginning of my career. I wasn't wearing a corporate suit, but a different kind of uniform.

My first day on the job, I walked into the Unit Headquarters wearing a freshly-starched battle dress uniform and brand-new spit-shined boots. I was a hotshot, the expert at everything, ready to give orders and command respect from my soldiers. My Company Commander greeted me and requested that I meet with my soldiers.

Following several hours of getting to know my soldiers, I noticed very few of them were actually speaking to me. Later in the day, my Platoon Sergeant who had over ten years of military service, called me over to his work station.

"Can I talk to you in private?" He then said something profound that altered the course of my career. "Sir, you are our Lieutenant, our platoon leader. You make the decisions. But…you still have to earn our respect."

As his words sunk in, I realized that if I was going to succeed as a leader, I couldn't do it alone. I didn't have to be good at everything, but I had to empower others while holding them accountable. In that initial role, I needed this Platoon Sergeant's full support and trust. He had the knowledge, experience, and respect of every soldier in the platoon. Even though I earned a leadership position and title, I still had a lot of work to do—and a lot to learn.

In that defining moment, I learned the meaning of leadership in the workplace. It is truly the art of influencing and bringing out the best in others to achieve a common goal, treating everyone with dignity and respect, regardless of their position.

And it doesn't just happen during your first day, week, month, or even your first year on the job. This level of leadership requires intentional effort over time. And that's why so few people at this stage take advantage of the opportunities to grow. They want to move up the ladder quickly, but, in their haste, actually slow their own growth.

Figuring It Out

The Exploration Stage is the time of early employment when an individual enters the workforce. The typical person in this stage usually has several fantasies and unrealistic expectations. Having not yet been jilted by the working world, they believe they will make the world a better place and be the change the world needs. I was the same way.

Like many college graduates just getting started, I believed that earning a Bachelor's Degree meant I was guaranteed a respectable salary and an executive position in Corporate America. Little did I know that my degree was only the price of admission. It got me a foot in the door, but that was it.

The lightbulb came on after Bobbie and I got married and I graduated from my ADA Officer Basic Course. When I got my first real paycheck with taxes taken out, I discovered there wasn't much money left. Not only that, but…surprise! I also didn't get to start at the top.

Nevertheless, as a 21-year-old, newly-commissioned 2nd Lieutenant in the US Army 1st Cavalry Division, I had a huge ego. I felt invincible, and acted like it, too. I had more than a slight chip on my shoulder, and I wore it proudly every day. After all, I had graduated in the top five of my ROTC graduating class at Jackson State University. I had been named top graduate of my officer basic course class. I believed that cliche: winning isn't everything; it's the only thing. I suppose I wasn't much different than most young, ambitious officers in the military, or the countless new hires I've seen in the corporate world over the decades.

To say I was impatient would be an understatement. I became a victim of the "I Want It Now" syndrome. It wasn't an easy pill to swallow that I wasn't appointed to every leadership position I wanted. When I didn't get picked, it really bothered me for quite a while. I felt that by graduating from college and my officer branch course with high marks, I was somehow entitled to be at the top or in key leadership roles.

However, after a seven-year career in the military, I ultimately learned that the necessary skills for being successful were persistence and patience. I came to understand that I wasn't ready and didn't have the experience others had who came before me, which was why I wasn't immediately put into advanced leadership positions. We won't be given the career-building projects and assignments from Day 1. Matriculation means learning to do the basics and asking the simple questions.

It took a while because I had to battle negative thoughts. Was I being held back because of the color of my skin? Did my commander just not like me? Unfortunately, I entertained all kinds of negative thinking. You may have experienced similar thoughts while relatively new in your career. The bottom line was, I needed to mature during that time but struggled to see it.

One thing I often failed to understand is that the Exploration Stage is the most forgiving stage of your career. My parents taught me to work twice as hard as everybody else, but I came to understand that it's okay to try hard and fail. It is not trying that is unacceptable. In fact, this stage of your career is an opportunity to fail early and often.

Everyone expects you to fall short when you are just starting, not so much once you reach the more advanced stages. As I came to understand this more, I consistently put in the hard work to be the best that I could be, utilize my God-given talent, and reach my full potential. Most importantly, I felt my time would come; it was only a matter of when it would happen.

A Straight Line Isn't Always Best

I worked my way through the Exploration Stage while I was in the military, but how would this stage look for a young person just getting started in a corporate environment or for an entrepreneur starting up a business? As a new entrant in the workforce, it's very important to understand career progression. How can you advance within your department? What is the company's organizational structure? What opportunities could there be outside of your department? What kind of time commitment will it take to get to the level you want to achieve? Will the guidance of a mentor be required to reach your goals?

Conversely, what do you need to learn as you grow this business? What mistakes can you afford to make? And are you preparing for the growth that will come as you succeed?

Once you understand the answers to these questions, you should be able to develop an idea of where you want to go and how to get there.

For example, if you're coming out of college and have accepted a job in the Human Resources field, generally the first position you'll get is HR Assistant, then HR Associate, then HR Manager, then HR Associate Director, then HR Director, then HR Vice-President. So you have to understand the organizational structure and the developmental requirements at each stage in order to get promoted. With most companies, unless they are a small organization, the career path is fairly well structured.

However, the path you take to get there is not necessarily linear. The shortest distance between two points is a straight line, but in the business world, you may have to move laterally or accept developmental assignments to expand your experience and build a solid career foundation. Often, when someone first enters the workforce, the primary focus is on the job position or title, rather than focusing on opportunities for growth, cross-training, in-depth learning, and development.

In the Exploration Stage, I eventually learned that what's most important is where you end up, not where you start. You have to be a lifelong learner. Absorb everything you can learn from the position you are in. Become an expert on as many positions as you can. This stage is your opportunity to soak up knowledge and experience, to try new things even if you fail occasionally. As long as you learn from mistakes, you'll grow from them.

One word of caution: New entrants into the workforce can be somewhat naive in thinking that all their colleagues or coworkers want to see them succeed. They may think, *Everyone is in my corner. Everyone wants to help me.* However, that's not how it works in corporate America, because in many cases you are competing with the people around you for positions. You have to learn who you can trust, who can give good advice, and who is a trusted team member.

That fact is part of what makes it so important to secure a mentor during this stage of your career. A mentor is someone to guide you and give you advice. A mentor is different from a sponsor, who is someone from within your company who chooses to help you advance. A mentor need not be in your company. In fact, at this stage, it's often more helpful to have someone who can offer you an outside perspective.

If you're new to the workforce, there are several methods you can use to find an appropriate mentor:

- Join professional organizations. When I join organizations locally and nationally, I seek out those who can give me good advice about the industry, my profession, my job function, and leadership in general.
- Connect with professionals on LinkedIn or other social media platforms.
- Ask a co-worker or colleague in the workplace whom you trust (this is key!) and has several years of service or experience ahead of you.
- Attend college or high school alumni events.
- Contact a prior college professor or high school teacher.
- Develop relationships in religious and community groups.

Wherever you find them, don't be afraid to ask for advice. The idea of grabbing coffee to gain professional advice is now the norm. The worst that someone can do is ignore your request or say no, but you'll never know if you don't reach out. Once the connection is made, you should set expectations upfront with your mentor on your goals for the relationship.

As I mentioned, you do need to keep a lookout when seeking a mentor from within your own company at this stage. The mentor/mentee relationship should not be forced. It should happen organically. It can't be based on the expectation of getting promoted or the appearance of favoritism.

You also have to be careful not to be labeled as incompetent, incapable, or someone who merely wants something handed to them. Always be prepared to put in long-term effort to get the job done. Getting a mentor to help advise you may accelerate your growth, but it is not a shortcut to get out of hard work.

Unfortunately, in most companies, new hires are expected to know how to navigate the corporate landscape. This expectation usually leads to anxiety and stress because you're left to figure it out on your own. There are a lot of unspoken rules you have to learn through trial and error, and failing to navigate them can derail you early in your career. That's why you can't be afraid to ask for help.

It's understandable that you might be nervous to ask for advice when entering a new role. You want to be perceived as knowing it all, but in reality, everyone knows you don't. You can easily become afraid to ask for help or admit you don't know something. But it's healthy to accept the reality that you don't know everything and are still learning.

You can't remain ignorant though. That's why you need to ask, quickly grasp the answers, learn the culture, and grow. But first, you have to ask. This is a great place for mentors. Demonstrating your abilities, asking the explicit questions, and creating a connection can build opportunities.

Master's or Mastery?

Should I get my Master's degree before entering the workforce? That's a question I get a lot from aspiring college grads.

Earning a Master's Degree is an awesome accomplishment. An advanced degree is usually required for upper management positions. However, without relevant experience to accompany the advanced degree, it doesn't necessarily equate to a higher salary or greater position of influence. The exception would be if you did an internship or had some sort of history with the company.

In general, I have found there's nothing more valuable than having a Bachelor's Degree and some experience before you earn your Master's, but it can also depend on the profession. If it's just a typical industry or company, I recommend getting your Bachelor's, getting some experience, then going for a Master's when you have the equivalent experience to go with it.

Your company may even be willing to pay for all or some of the tuition in that case. I recommend any person in Stage

1 of the Career Life Cycle look at the different companies' benefits for those who would pay for your Master's or your Doctorate down the road. For example, Kraft paid for my MBA about ten years into my career. I could have gotten it earlier, but because I was moving through the organization so fast, I didn't have time.

You choose which path is right for you, but more education without real-world experience may not produce the greatest growth when you're in the Exploration Stage of the Career Life Cycle.

Leadership Competencies

At each stage of the Career Life Cycle, individuals should have developed certain Leadership Competencies, which are skills and behaviors that contribute to superior performance. Your competency in—or ability to show—these skills will increase the trust that your team and your superiors have in you.

Though there are wide-ranging examples of Leadership Competencies, the five we will focus on for each stage of the Career Life Cycle are Personal / Interpersonal Skills, Drive, Strategic Skills, Operating Skills, and Professionalism.

Leadership Competencies in Stage 1: Exploration

PERSONAL / INTERPERSONAL SKILLS:

Demonstrating self-awareness; self-development

- ✓ You are aware of your impact on others, as well as knowing yourself well and acknowledging that you have some blind spots.
- ✓ You reflect on what you have done, seek feedback, and are open to ways to improve.
- ✓ You are able to effectively communicate with others.

DRIVE:

Action-oriented; drives results

- ✓ You have a strong sense of immediacy, focusing on the task at hand and seeing it through to completion.
- ✓ You consistently achieve results, even under tough circumstances.

STRATEGIC SKILLS:

Business insight; mental agility

- ✓ You combine data and analysis to find meaning in and increase understanding of a situation, resulting in some competitive advantage for your business. This provides more than just a low-level understanding of an issue.

- ✓ You are able to think on your feet, solve problems, and are creative at work.
- ✓ You are able to understand workflow and compliance and/or safety initiatives.
- ✓ You are able to lead with confidence such that others will follow you.

OPERATING SKILLS:

Plans and aligns; organizational savvy

- ✓ You are skilled at planning and prioritizing work to meet commitments aligned with organizational goals.
- ✓ You have become aware of and familiar with the often unspoken areas of organizational life, such as power dynamics, competing agendas, perceptions, turf issues, self-promotion, trust, and relationships.
- ✓ You can achieve results to prove your abilities.

PROFESSIONALISM:

Situational adaptability

- ✓ You are aware of the complexities in a given situation and can be flexible and act differently when required because no two situations are exactly alike.

CHAPTER 3

STAGE 2—ESTABLISHMENT

Stage 2 of the Career Life Cycle is the Establishment phase. At this critical stage, an individual is given opportunities to demonstrate agility, make mistakes, deliver results, lead at different levels, and receive promotions in positions of greater responsibility. In some cases, the individual may be assigned a mentor or coach to assist in career development and advancement. In other cases, the individual may have to seek out such support.

My Establishment Stage occurred from 1991-1999, a time which included my last two years in the military, and then working for Kraft, two years in Madison and five years in South Carolina. I was always learning, test driving things, and volunteering.

After passing several "tests" and gaining my coworkers' trust, doors of opportunity started to open. After one year of service, the General Manager in Madison called me to his office and asked if he could be my mentor. That was a pivotal moment.

This is a phenomenon in which your supervisor sees your potential, maybe even seeing a bit of themself in you and your work. You begin to create a reputation that will precede you throughout your career.

As my mentor, the General Manager required that he and I have a face-to-face meeting each month. He gave me monthly assignments to complete and required that I give him an update on what I had learned and accomplished.

Having a mentor doesn't mean that he or she owes you a promotion or that you will get more opportunities. It is a chance for you to come alongside someone who can offer objective insights into what steps you might take and habits you might adopt to help you on your career journey.

I was fortunate that soon after I started working with my mentor—just a few weeks—I was promoted to a Financial Analyst position. We continued our mentor/mentee relationship, and I embraced and applied the wisdom and advice he so generously shared. After two years at the company, I was promoted to a Senior Financial Analyst position, which required relocating to South Carolina. At that moment, I realized something magical was happening, and the hard work was paying off.

Making Mistakes

At the Establishment Stage of the Career Life Cycle, you're still learning, growing, and making mistakes. If I was feeling a little too big for my britches because of this promotion, I was very soon brought back to reality.

My degree is in finance, not accounting. Yes, I took accounting classes in college, but I was far better at analyzing financial results and understanding where the gains and losses were coming from than actually doing the accounting in journal ledgers.

However, not wanting to appear ignorant or incapable on any level, when a situation occurred that required some ledger work, I went ahead and tried to do what I thought I was supposed to, rather than asking the Plant Controller for help.

When the end of the month arrived, and it was time to close out the books, I found out just how bad a move that was. About 7:00 pm on what was already turning into a late night, the Controller came out of his office and said, "I wish we could be finished, but someone did a bad entry and we're $50,000 short."

I made the connection right away. I had messed up. I started sweating bullets, thinking I was about to lose my job. This guy was rigid, as are most accountants. So I had to go in and own up to it. "I have some bad news. I'm the one who screwed up that entry. I must have put the numbers in the wrong columns."

He checked it, and after we spent a couple of hours looking for the entry and how it impacted the bottom line, it was clear how I had screwed up. I had a team of analysts who worked for me who were good at this sort of thing—and I should have recognized that fact and handed the task over.

I probably lost some credibility that day, but at least I didn't lose my job. In some fields and organizations, mistakes are encouraged. It is in these mistakes that we learn the most valuable lessons. There is still some room for error during the Establishment Stage, and I was certainly grateful for it.

Learning Agility

With my success and failures, I was learning—and learning agility is a key component of the Establishment Stage. You must be willing to take risks, be vulnerable, and be prepared to fail early and often. Additionally, you have to aggressively seek out development opportunities and assignments. You have to be strategic in seeking "key" growth opportunities that will enhance your skills and abilities.

You also must be willing to work quietly, without recognition and accolades. This may happen when you are embarking on a path that hasn't been taken before. Others may even judge you for the work you're doing, but that's because they don't know or believe in your dream.

That's basically what I did. I felt empowered to try things, to take risks. At one point, my manager sat down with me and asked where I wanted to be in twenty years. He said, "I want to help you get there, wherever it is you want to be." I put two things on that list: VP of Finance or VP of Human Resources. I believed I could do it. I had a vision. My manager told me he would do all he could to help me achieve it. I was eager to learn, so I was given opportunities. At this stage, it's critical to get your manager's and leadership team's support.

I consider myself to be a lifelong learner. I was always inquisitive, adventurous, creative, and never hesitant in providing my perspective. Additionally, I felt that my life purpose was to actively seek opportunities to be a trailblazer—I wanted to be first! I really never thought that I had reached my full potential. As a result, I did not accept complacency. And, yes, I was somewhat impatient.

When experiencing new or unfamiliar situations, I would always ask Why questions to gain a better understanding of situations, problems, or opportunities. Then, I would follow up with Who, What, When, Where, and How questions.

Learning was a skill I picked up in the military, probably due to the training I went through as an officer. They put you through scenarios where you have to think and plan for the future with Plan A, Plan B, and Plan C, and more. Back then, I didn't know this type of thinking was called Learning Agility, but I've always loved the principle; I love what it does.

At this stage, you should be a lifelong learner, always wanting to stay fresh, stay competitive, and challenge yourself. So I'd recommend this as a time to consider an advanced degree. If you are worried about whether or not you have time, you simply have to make a commitment, exercising dedication and discipline.

Even if you aren't at a place where you can consider additional schooling, commit to learning, always. The practice of reading the newest, relevant research and information will give you a leading edge.

You must have a conversation with your manager—not to get his or her approval, because that's your business, but you want your manager's support. You want his or her blessing. There will be times when you have to take off work early or need some help with things, so you'll want that support. Get your manager's vote of confidence.

Ideally, you will work for a company that pays for that degree, as I did. But if getting an advanced degree is what you really want to do, with or without the company's support, do it. Do it for yourself. At some point, if you decide to leave the company and you have your Master's degree, it will help you at the next company. In fact, for some companies, it's the price of admission.

This Establishment Stage may not always feel like the right time to go after a Master's degree. In most cases, the next stage, the Elevation Stage, is the better stage to do it, because you've been around long enough that you have more practical experience to go along with the degree.

Leadership Competencies in Stage 2: Establishment

Leadership Competencies continue to build over the course of your career. The competencies of Stage 2 include continued development of the competencies introduced in Stage 1, as well as the addition of new skills and abilities.

PERSONAL / INTERPERSONAL SKILLS:

Self-awareness, interpersonal savvy, builds networks

- ✓ You build and maintain solid working relationships with colleagues, superiors, and direct reports.
- ✓ You continue to enhance skills such as good listening, empathy, honesty, sincerity, a strong orientation toward teamwork, trustworthiness, supportiveness, and a willingness to share responsibility.
- ✓ You develop formal and informal relationship networks inside and outside the organization.
- ✓ You are so knowledgeable about your field that you become someone colleagues turn to for answers.

DRIVE:

Drives results, resiliency

- ✓ You adjust to change, whatever the circumstances may be, and navigate all the ups and downs and twists and turns on your career path.

- ✓ You persist in the face of challenges and setbacks.
- ✓ You always keep the end in sight; put in extra effort to meet deadlines.

STRATEGIC SKILLS:

Business insights, mental agility

- ✓ You consistently apply a business driver and marketplace focus when prioritizing actions.
- ✓ You are the first to spot possible future policies, practices, and trends in the organization, with the competition, and in the marketplace.

OPERATING SKILLS:

Plans and aligns, decision quality, communicates effectively

- ✓ You actively seek input from pertinent sources to make timely and well-informed decisions—even the toughest ones.
- ✓ You think critically and make high-quality decisions, even when based on incomplete information or in the face of uncertainty.
- ✓ You develop and deliver multi-mode communications that convey a clear understanding of the unique needs of different audiences.

PROFESSIONALISM:

Situational adaptability, courage

- ✓ You pick up on the need to change personal, interpersonal, and leadership behaviors quickly.
- ✓ You address difficult issues, saying what needs to be said.

CHAPTER 4

STAGE 3—ELEVATION

At this third stage of the Career Life Cycle, you will have been in the game long enough to understand how it's played and to have earned a seat at the table. In most cases at this stage, it's simply unacceptable to fail to deliver results or to add value to the company on a daily basis.

You have proven in the previous Establishment Stage that you're learning agile, ambitious, and can deliver results. Stage 3 is the time to challenge your confidence and put your knowledge to the test. At this stage, you must have confidence in your own skills/abilities, be able to deliver top-tier business results, be comfortable competing with the best-of-the-best, and thrive on being in charge and leading people.

You are part of, or lead, a high-functioning team. The results you have produced added value to your field in some capacity. Overall, you become a trusted resource for others.

That said, it is also critically important to understand the business, have functional expertise, understand technical processes, embrace diversity, and get things accomplished by delegating to other people and teams. In order to be successful in the Elevation Stage of your career, you must have a strong foundation and meaningful experiences in the Establishment Stage.

The bottom line is this: if you don't handle this stage well, there won't be a Stage 4. I'm not trying to be an alarmist, but Stage 3 is the most critical stage; if you don't make it here, you're done. You've had the opportunity to fail in earlier stages, but doing so in the Elevation Stage could derail your career.

By this point, you must have embraced the reality that you are the CEO of your own career. You more than likely have an assigned sponsor and should be on track for promotion at least two levels above your current salary. If you've put in the time, worked hard, made connections, and delivered consistent results, you're probably considered to be a top talent at the company. Because of your experience, accolades, and elevated position, you will also likely have a mentee at this stage that will come along behind you in their own career cycle.

If you are an entrepreneur, your business has likely grown to a level of stability, and you'll need to make decisions as to how far you want it to grow and in which direction. You'll likely need to make trade-offs and choose key people to help lead the company for years ahead as it outgrows your ability to manage it all yourself.

At this stage, it's essential to balance career and personal life, because a lot will likely be asked of you in both directions. Plus, you should be well on your way with retirement savings, wealth building through 401k or other retirement vehicles, stocks, and personal savings.

Nothing Comes Easy

Some people have the misconception that the higher you climb on the business success ladder, the easier it gets. You imagine you'll just sit back and let those lower than you on the ladder do all the heavy lifting. The reality is just the opposite. The higher your position, the more responsibility you have, so by the Elevation Stage, you can expect to face challenging situations regularly. In fact, it's a time you have to consider the tradeoffs in your personal life you may need to make to keep moving up to the C-Suite.

I asked fifty colleagues from a variety of positions and backgrounds for three key challenges they faced. The number one most common challenge was burnout. They work long hours to prove themselves; the phone never stops ringing; they have to be first in last out, and it takes a toll on them.

The second biggest challenge was work/life balance. While focusing on achieving the next promotion, they often have to spend less time focused on their families, their relationships, or even their hobbies. They can't go to kids' sporting events, can't be there to cook dinner, can't run errands. Sometimes it feels easier at this stage to be in the office than at home since at the office, you at least have people you can delegate to.

The third most common challenge was career advancement. At this stage, they hit a brick wall because they felt like they were doing all they needed to do from a performance standpoint and meeting expectations, but there was no career path or advancement. At that point, people jump ship. They feel no loyalty from the company, so they go somewhere else where they can potentially earn more and get the advancement.

In the Elevation Stage of the Career Life Cycle, it's a good idea to keep your options open. Keep a finger on the pulse of the marketplace, talk to headhunters, and do interviews so you always know your worth. Keep your name out there, because you never know what tomorrow will bring. Never close the windows of opportunity.

The same is true for entrepreneurs. Always be open to new opportunities as you grow your business. You just never know what opportunities may develop when you have the mindset to look out for them.

The Succession Plan

If you are in the corporate world, most companies have a Succession Plan that is reviewed and discussed by senior leaders in the organization on an annual basis, usually late in the 3rd Quarter or early in the 4th Quarter. Individuals are not placed on the Succession Plan until they've reached a certain job title or pay scale level.

Your manager and/or Human Resources should inform you of the process and let you know where you are on the Succession Plan. Your manager should have a career or talent planning conversation with you annually or semi-annually.

At this point, having a sponsor is extremely valuable. A sponsor is different from a coach or mentor. Rather than guiding and directing you on a regular basis, your sponsor is usually assigned to you or volunteers to be your corporate godfather, sometimes even without your knowledge. This sponsor might be a corporate executive, a division chief, a tenured professor, a department chair, or other roles, depending on your industry.

This person has a seat in the room when senior leaders are discussing who gets promoted or assigned to key and critical positions within the company, and will advocate on your behalf. They function like an invisible hand guiding the process.

Being placed on the Succession Plan generally happens when you reach a certain level in management and is typically based on potential and performance. It may be that you're well-placed where you currently are, or you may be considered top talent, the best and the brightest, and will be slotted for upward mobility.

At the Elevation Stage, you should be on the Succession Plan to be promoted to at least two levels above your current salary grade. When you rise to senior manager level, if no one is telling you that your name is listed on the Succession Plan, or your manager is not discussing succession planning with you, my advice is to ask.

When you sit down with your manager for your annual evaluation, ask directly if you are on the Succession Plan. Ask if you are looked upon as top talent, someone who has legs or a skillset to go higher up in the organization.

In my experience, if you're really doing what you need to do and are considered among the best and brightest, you really don't have to ask; they'll seek you out. But there are some people who are on the bubble, right in the middle, and don't really know their future. If this is the case, you may not be on the Plan, but you can't be afraid to ask.

If you've made it to that senior level, you must be courageous and ask your manager the tough questions. If you're a senior leader who doesn't feel comfortable asking if you are on the Plan, then you probably aren't.

If you do ask and find you're not on the Plan, you'll have to have a difficult conversation with your manager. Ask what he or she sees as your next opportunity. Does he or she see you having different opportunities or greater responsibilities in the organization? You can still have a good career if you understand that the likelihood of your moving up is slim, but you can move around laterally.

But at some point in your career, especially if you know you're not going anywhere, you might have to make the tough individual decision that it's time to move on.

Leadership Competencies in Stage 3: Elevation

PERSONAL / INTERPERSONAL SKILLS:

Collaborates, values differences

- ✓ You build partnerships and work collaboratively with others to meet shared objectives.
- ✓ You recognize the value that different perspectives and cultures bring to an organization.

DRIVE:

Optimizes work processes, nimble learning

- ✓ You know the most effective and efficient processes to get things done, with a focus on continuous improvement.
- ✓ You actively learn through experimentation when tackling new problems, using both successes and failures.

STRATEGIC SKILLS:

Mental agility, learning agility, strategic mindset, cultivates innovation

- ✓ You see ahead to future possibilities and translate them into breakthrough strategies.
- ✓ You map out aggressive steps that will clearly accelerate the organization toward its strategic goals.
- ✓ You create new and better ways for the organization to be successful.

OPERATING SKILLS:

Dealing with complexity, change agility, delegation

- ✓ You make sense of complex, high-quality, and sometimes contradictory information to effectively solve problems.
- ✓ You address new challenges as they present themselves, rapidly implement and integrate new learning or practices, and even change an entire direction resourcefully within a short space of time.
- ✓ You provide direction, delegate, and remove obstacles to get work done.
- ✓ You convey clear performance expectations and follow up consistently.

PROFESSIONALISM:

Manages ambiguity

- ✓ You operate effectively, even when things are not certain or the way forward is not clear.
- ✓ You adapt quickly to changing conditions.

CHAPTER 5

STAGE 4—ENRICHMENT

During the Enrichment Stage, you'll reach the highest position possible based on your career trajectory and promotability within the company, whether it is the company you started or an international corporation.

At this stage, unfortunately, in many cases, position and salary stagnation occur, as there simply are not many higher positions for advancement. The air starts to get pretty thin. When you realize you're not going to be promoted further, or you've grown as far as you can in that environment, you have two options: stay and make the best of it or take a job with a different company where you can advance further.

If you stay, seek ways to remain relevant and add value. Ask yourself what you have done for the company lately. Do your best to have a strong professional relationship with your manager. People tend to see the company through the lens of their bosses or managers, and they stay or go because of that relationship, more than for the company itself.

Let's face it—at this stage of your career, ageism can become a concern. Age 55 and 10 years of service are important numbers, particularly as it relates to a reduction in workforce, cost savings, and the company's bottom line. One situation in which this may not be true is in the medical world or academia, where age equals clout and retirement is pushed until later.

Therefore, you can't stick your head in the sand to try not to deal with the inevitable. At some point in life, you will begin to reach the sunset of your career.

However, that doesn't prevent you from focusing your efforts and attention on remaining relevant, exceeding performance expectations, and being a subject-matter expert. Not only can doing this make your journey fulfilling, but in some industries, employees are also staying in the workforce longer and often adding value with their technical knowledge, professional maturity, and ability to mentor/bring along younger professionals.

If you decide to leave, you must have a plan for your next move immediately. At this stage, you should always have a transition plan and an exit strategy ready because you don't know when you may be invited to leave. An option may be mentorship programs, consulting, or stepping into the research realm.

If you haven't yet met with a financial advisor, it's definitely time. By this point, you need to know your target for retirement savings, both the dollar amount and the year you want to retire. Your trusted and certified financial planner will help you make sure you're where you should be.

Also during this career peak, you should become a mentor to help guide others through their career experiences and challenges. Spend time developing others to get them ready for promotions. I was very intentional in leaving a legacy through others and ensuring the company was seeded with the best and brightest talent.

During and prior to this stage, I aggressively sought mentees who were eager to learn, willing to put in the work, and committed to reaching their full potential as human resources professionals. I felt responsible for the future of the company, as well as the viability of the human resources function. I mentored several successful HR Professionals, some of whom are still with the company, and others who left for external promotional opportunities.

You'll also begin to prepare for life after your corporate career, laying the foundation for the life you want to live when that day comes.

Learn to Read the Tea Leaves

In the Enrichment Stage, you are getting closer to meeting the retirement threshold. During this stage, it's critical that you pay attention to the signs that reveal themselves—read the tea leaves, so to speak.

If you are in a corporate environment, understand how the company operates, both its written and unwritten rules. Be attentive—know what's going on in the business and in your industry. Understand and know the details regarding major company changes, such as mergers, acquisitions, divestitures, and workforce reductions.

Participate in the quarterly or annual company earnings meeting to gain a better understanding of the state of the company. You will be surprised by what you learn and the bits of knowledge discussed.

At this point, you are expected to be a subject matter expert (SME) and the go-to person in the company, or for your brand if you are an entrepreneur. You have long-tenured experience and a broad professional network. Your productivity should be at an all-time high with high ticket results. Maybe your research is contributing to your field in an impactful way. The company is expecting a Return on Investment (ROI). You will have to show your value and worth.

Remember that you're nearing the twilight of your career; therefore, you have to remain relevant to the changes in your business or technical environment. It's more about continued professional development rather than functional expertise, which you should already have.

My focus at this stage turned to leaving a legacy with my direct reports, colleagues, and company. I became even more intentional about leaving behind a nurturing culture—a family atmosphere that's a great place to work. I would ask myself daily, "Who can I share with? Who can I help?"

This stage is also a time where you have the margin to truly make yourself a top priority. Take time to schedule meetings with your Financial Advisor. Take time off with your family. Maybe there are some places you've dreamed of taking them to. You may now have the financial ability and accrued vacation to do so.

Where to Next?

As you start thinking about life after your current company, whether moving on to another employer, starting your own business, or retiring, there are some resources you can and should use to help you get on the right track.

If you're looking for further employment, research a good resume writer to help you get your resume ready for distribution. Write your resume to keep the focus off your age, and highlight your outstanding qualifications and experience. Make sure your professional online profile (i.e. LinkedIn) is current and up-to-date. If you haven't created one yet, it may be a good idea to recruit someone to help you with that. (If you have young adult children, they're a great place to start!)

Maybe you've dreamed of starting your own business—exactly what I did! The Small Business Administration is a great resource for those just getting started.

If you know that retirement is your next step, then this stage is when it's important to start getting those ducks in a row. One of the first things to do is schedule a meeting with HR and the Benefits Provider to better understand pre-retirement topics, including the company's benefits package, pension, and 401k.

You'll also want to do your research, meet with experts, and ask questions about the following: financial planning, retirement planning, social security, tax laws, best places to live for retirees, and how to stay active physically and mentally.

Do not lock yourself inside a bubble. Connect with other people who are close to retirement, retired, or in a similar situation. Plan to spend some time together or establish a support group.

Whatever you do, don't get caught in a depressive state thinking about your career coming to an end. Get out of that space quickly—if you're intentional, the best is yet to come!

Leadership Competencies in Stage 4: Enrichment

PERSONAL / INTERPERSONAL SKILLS:

Communicates effectively

- ✓ You model and encourage the expression of diverse ideas and opinions.
- ✓ You adjust communication content and style to meet the needs of diverse stakeholders.

DRIVE:

Resourcefulness

- ✓ You secure and deploy resources effectively and efficiently.
- ✓ You get the most out of available resources and locate rare resources others can't get.
- ✓ You adapt quickly to changing resource requirements.

STRATEGIC SKILLS:

Mental agility, strategic mindset, managing vision and purpose

- ✓ You paint a compelling picture of the vision and strategy that motivates others to action.
- ✓ You instill and sustain organization-wide energy for what is possible.
- ✓ You show personal commitment to the vision.

OPERATING SKILLS:

Develops talent, ensures accountability

✓ You view talent development as an organizational imperative.

✓ You consistently use multiple methods to develop others.

✓ You promote a sense of urgency and establish and enforce individual accountability in the team.

✓ You work with people to establish explicit performance standards.

PROFESSIONALISM:

Approachability

✓ You keep your tone warm and friendly, maintain eye contact, and don't get distracted.

✓ You listen to what a person has to say without interrupting them.

✓ You pay attention to your body language.

CHAPTER 6

STAGE 5—EXIT

You have a choice at the Exit Stage of the Career Life Cycle. You can either prepare to exit with dignity and on your own terms, or you can slip into decline. In the Exit Stage, the decision has been made, either by you or the company, that it's time to part ways, either voluntarily or involuntarily. If you're not prepared to step away from your corporate career and into what's next, this can be the most difficult stage. But it doesn't have to be. It certainly wasn't for me. You may choose to retire or reinvent yourself to remain viable in the workforce. Or both.

Here are some indicators that you've reached your peak in the company:

- Fewer opportunities are coming your way, and you sense a lack of promotability.
- You feel like you're not in the inner circle or circle of influence.
- You're not able to read the tea leaves because they're not giving you any tea leaves to read; you're out of the loop.

- You wake up in the morning, and you're not happy to go into the office or regret getting up to go to work.
- You really don't care about the company or your managers.

The Unplanned Exit

If the day comes when you are approached and informed that your job is being terminated, here are some things to keep in mind.

First, ask why the situation is happening. From a mental standpoint, it's important to understand so you can bring closure to your tenure with the company. Ask if the exit being presented to you is voluntary or involuntary. Do you have a choice in the matter?

If it is voluntary, then you have to do some soul searching about whether or not you wish to stay with a company that may not keep you around much longer. At the very least, you will want to get your resume updated and put out some feelers if you choose to stay on.

When the exit is not voluntary, do your research and confirm if a severance package is being offered to exit the company. This package is not required, but it is a nice gesture by the company. With big companies, a severance package may consist of up to a year's pay, bonuses, stocks, cash-out of accrued PTO, professional transition services, and continued insurance for a period of time.

These days, as companies tighten their financial belts, a severance package is more likely to consist of two weeks of pay, whatever vacation you had coming, and COBRA healthcare coverage.

If some sort of severance compensation is offered, get a clear understanding of the total payout amount and benefits details, especially around healthcare insurance. Confirm the timing of the total payout amount due to tax implications. In other words, will the money be paid out in the current year or the following year, and will the payment be in a lump sum or dispersed during the regular payroll cycle? If it's paid during the regular payroll cycle, how many payments will be received? If a severance package is not offered, don't be afraid to ask for one. You have nothing to lose but everything to gain.

Find out if Professional Outplacement Services will be included in the severance package. This service will assist you and your spouse in transitioning and may include help with the job search, resume writing, and additional training.

Consult with an attorney and your financial advisor. When you get the severance package, there's often a severance and general release agreement that confirms the company is going to let you go, and, in return, is going to give you a certain amount of money or benefits. You'll be asked to sign this document saying you aren't going to sue them. If you don't sign the document, you don't get the package.

If you didn't read the tea leaves and you find yourself without a job late in your career, unprepared for the loss, there are some damage mitigation steps you can take. You may have to decide if you're going to officially retire and draw your pension, or if you're going to continue to work. It's important to discuss this with a financial advisor first to understand all the financial ramifications.

If you decide not to retire, then apply for unemployment benefits at your local unemployment office. Meanwhile, as you start a new job hunt...

Update your resume. Seek assistance from an employment agency or recruiter.

Leverage your professional network. Update your social media sites. Review and analyze your skills inventory.

Your unplanned exit is obviously going to impact your family, so I recommend scheduling family counseling to help you work through the transition, which can include a reduction in unnecessary spending and possibly downsizing, if necessary. It won't be an easy time for you or your family.

If the unplanned termination is thrust upon you, don't become the victim. Own it. Accept the exit. You'll be stronger by letting go and focusing on the future. Not letting go creates anxiety in several ways—mentally, emotionally, and financially—and it's just not worth it.

What's Next?

Many people have to work well into their 60s for their social security benefits and other financial reasons. This could put them in the Exit Stage for longer than ten years. Is it possible to have a meaningful work life when you're waiting longer to retire? Absolutely!

In that extended scenario, I would say you are extending the Enrichment Stage rather than moving to the Exit Stage and lingering there. You'll want to seize every opportunity to stay relevant by continuing to learn and grow in your role. Becoming a mentor is really a must-do in this scenario; you have much wisdom and experience to share, and the pleasure you'll gain by helping those behind you reach even greater heights is immeasurable.

However, you should definitely be using the extra time to ensure you are totally prepared to exit the company on your own when the time comes, following all the guidelines I shared in the previous chapter. And you have to stay prepared for the unexpected termination discussed above; remember, the company doesn't love you and is probably not concerned with whether or not you are financially ready to go. Your financial future is simply not a priority for the company. Be accountable for your own destiny.

Whether you retire, exit intentionally, or are simply let go without notice, the day will come when you wake up without your day job and think, *Now What?!*

First and foremost, it is a golden opportunity to spend some quality time with friends and family. If your financial situation is compromised, then don't worry about things like meeting up for lunch or playing an expensive round of golf; invite them over for a cup of coffee. Host a pot-luck dinner.

You can have fun together and enjoy one another's company without breaking the bank.

Volunteer your time and services to organizations you care about, including nonprofits, churches, etc. I mentioned in the last chapter that I offered to serve on the boards of some organizations that are important to me. Your wisdom and expertise at this stage of your career may be exactly what a charity or other non-profit organization needs.

Connect with others in your age group or similar situations. In my case, when I exited the company, I really didn't know what to do. I was feeling a little lost. One day, I went to the golf course on a weekday and was a little surprised to find that there were actually many other people out there. I was by myself, and the only black person out there that time of day. A group of guys called out, "Hey—who are you? Are you golfing by yourself? Come on and golf with us!"

As we got to talking, I shared that I was recently retired. These guys, all older and also retired, started to tease me about being too young to be retired. They also discovered that my golf game wasn't exactly up to par.

That was many months ago. Now, every Monday and Thursday our group has a set tee-time. These guys have really taken me under their collective wing, and we have become friends. I'm learning things from them about golf and about retired life. They've become like friends.

Leadership Competencies in Stage 5: Exit

PERSONAL / INTERPERSONAL SKILLS:

Self-awareness, self-development

- ✓ You take consistent action to develop new skills that may serve beyond your current career.
- ✓ You are aware of the skills needed to be successful in different situations.

DRIVE:

Ambition, nimble learning

- ✓ You enjoy the challenge of unfamiliar tasks.
- ✓ You seek new approaches to solve problems.
- ✓ You identify and seize new opportunities.

STRATEGIC SKILLS:

Mental agility, strategic mindset, business insight

- ✓ You have an in-depth understanding of how businesses work and make money.
- ✓ You formulate a clear strategy and map the steps that will clearly accelerate you toward your post-exit goals.

OPERATING SKILLS:

Cultivates innovation

- ✓ You move beyond traditional ways of doing things and/or push past the status quo.
- ✓ You explore new, creative options for utilizing your skills.

PROFESSIONALISM:

Manages conflict

- ✓ You anticipate conflicts before they happen based on knowledge of interpersonal and group dynamics.
- ✓ You find common ground and drive to consensus, ensuring that all feel heard.

CHAPTER 7

FINAL THOUGHTS

At the time of this writing, in mid-2022, I think we can all agree the last couple of years have been as unpredictable as any we've ever lived. And yet, despite the challenges, pivots, and uncertainties, thanks to my many years of dedication to the Career Life Cycle and my careful Stage 5 Exit plans, my new venture C and B HR Consulting is thriving.

After a career spent honing my expertise in Human Resources, we decided to create an HR consulting firm that will help our business clients reach their full potential by building incredible, diverse teams and leaders. I consider it not just another job, but a calling, almost a ministry, to give back and inspire others.

There is something extra sweet about partnering with new businesses who are excited to learn about the solutions we can offer to help them grow their business and develop their people, but who also become our valued friends. That level of relationship and partnership is what I dreamed of when we started this firm as a side-hustle, and I'm looking forward to living that dream through the remainder of my working years.

My goal for this book is to be a beacon of hope for readers. If I could succeed in my career, even coming from my very humble beginnings, surely you can as well. The true test of a person's success is not just looking at where the journey started, but where it ends. With the right attitude, faith, and a lot of hard work, you can accomplish amazing things—things you may never have even dreamed were possible. Believe in yourself and aim high.

But you can't get there alone. In all my years interacting with people at the highest level of their career, not one has reached that point without plenty of help along the way, and my hope is that you will take the guidance offered in these pages to help you through the remaining stages of your Career Life Cycle, too.

If you're a leader in your organization and want your people to understand the Career Life Cycle and mindset, I would be honored to have a conversation with you about how you can leverage the concepts shared in this book to grow your business and team.

Just visit CBHRconsulting.com and send me a note.

ABOUT THE AUTHOR

Charles L. Jones (US Army Captain, Veteran) is principal of C&B HR Consulting and a seasoned Human Resource Executive with over 25 years of experience in Human Resources and Manufacturing Operations in Fortune 500 companies like Kraft and Mondelez International. He and his team provide human resources strategies and solutions to a wide range of businesses and nonprofits including Intel, YWCA, and Millennium Corporation.

Learn more at CBHRconsulting.com.

This work reflects the author's present recollections of his experiences over time. Occasionally, dialogue consistent with the character or nature of the person speaking has been supplemented. Some names and characteristics have been changed out of a respect for privacy and some events have been abridged. Names, characters, places, and incidents are based on the author's memories, where others may have conflicting memories. The intent of this work is to encourage the reader to move forward in their career and life, no matter the adversity or obstacles that come their way.

Made in the USA
Monee, IL
05 February 2023

27163155R00039